CYBER
WARS

MATT ANNISS

Cavendish
Square

New York

Published in 2018 by Cavendish Square Publishing, LLC
243 5th Avenue, Suite 136, New York, NY 10016

Website: cavendishsq.com

This publication represents the opinions and views of the author based on his or her personal experience, knowledge, and research. The information in this book serves as a general guide only. The author and publisher have used their best efforts in preparing this book and disclaim liability rising directly or indirectly from the use and application of this book.

All websites were available and accurate when this book was sent to press.

Library of Congress Cataloging-in-Publication Data

Names: Anniss, Matt.
Title: Cyber wars / Matt Anniss.
Description: New York : Cavendish Square, 2018. | Series: I witness war | Includes index. | Audience: Grades 5–8.
Identifiers: ISBN 9781502632579 (library bound) | ISBN 9781502634344 (pbk.) | ISBN 9781502633279 (ebook)
Subjects: LCSH: Information warfare—Juvenile literature. | Cyberterrorism—Juvenile literature. | Computer security—Juvenile literature. | National security—Juvenile literature.
Classification: LCC U163.A56 2018 | DDC 355.4—dc23

Produced for Cavendish Square by Calcium
Editors: Sarah Eason and Jennifer Sanderson
Designers: Paul Myerscough and Simon Borrough
Picture Researcher: Rachel Blount

Picture credits: Cover: Shutterstock: Joe Prachatree; Inside: Shutterstock: Africa Studio 31, Andrey Popov 13, Andrey VP 12, Asharkyu 4, Astrelok 34, BeeBright 17, Billion Photos 15, ChameleonsEye 42, Dariush M 28, Chistoprudov Dmitriy 32, Drop of Light 21, Evan El-Amin 38, Emel82 29, Everett Historical 6, F8 Studio 41, FabrikaSimf 33, Richard Frazier 37, GongTo 24, Rob Kints 36, Thomas Koch 14, Kojoku 18, 19, Ksander 44, Lazyllama 35, Frederic Legrand – COMEO 43, lOvE lOvE 30, Mikhail 11, Volodymyr Nikitenko 9, Osugi 26, Joe Prachatree 45, ProStockStudio 1, 22, Redpixel.pl 5, Galina Savina 40, Vladimir Sazonov 16, Rena Schild 25, Stock Photo World 39, Syda Productions 7, Turtix 23, Victority 10, Nickolay Vinokurov 20; Wikimedia Commons: Violaine Martin 27, Bob McNeely, The White House 8.

Printed in the United States of America

CONTENTS

CHAPTER 1

WHAT IS CYBER WARFARE?

In the twenty-first century, wars are not fought only on battlefields with guns and bombs, at sea with fleets of battleships and submarines, or from the air using helicopter gunships and fighter jets. Today, there is another threat to our security and that of others around the world.

The fighters in this new conflict are not very visible. They hide in the shadows, covering their tracks to make it almost impossible to confirm their identities. Their weapons are not rifles, tanks, or machine guns, but computers. Their targets can vary, from leading businesses and important individuals to governments and even the power plants that provide us with electricity. From behind a computer keyboard, they are capable of launching attacks at the click of a mouse, from anywhere in the world. They are known as computer hackers, and they are the foot soldiers of a new type of conflict: cyber warfare.

As cyber warfare is on the rise, governments and large companies have to take their computer security very seriously.

Hackers use their programming skills to gain access to another person's computer files over the Internet.

The battlefield of cyber war is the Internet, the global **network** that connects billions of devices around the world. Those who take part in cyber warfare can target any device connected to the Internet, whether it is a personal computer, the specialist computers that run websites, known as servers, or your smartphone. At the end of 2016, around 3.4 billion people worldwide regularly connected to the Internet. That figure will continue to rise as technology is developed. This means that there are millions of potential targets for anyone intent on waging cyber war. It is also easier for hackers to hide and cover their tracks, making it difficult to bring them to justice.

The world of cyber warfare is an incredibly secretive one. Few hackers will admit that they are responsible for attacks. Many governments around the world will acknowledge that they have special units to deal with cyberattacks, but almost all deny using cyber warfare to spy on their enemies, let alone attack them with sophisticated new cyberweapons. We know about some acts of cyber warfare through the work of investigative journalists, former spies, a few brave witnesses, and dedicated cybersecurity experts. All of these individuals have risked their lives to alert the world to the growing threat of cyberattacks.

In 1962, a computer science researcher named J. C. R. Licklider wrote a report proposing a new "galactic network" of interconnected computers. Licklider thought it would be possible to share information between computers in different parts of the world using the existing telephone networks. He was correct. Over the years and decades that followed, this international network grew and became known as the Internet. As technology improved, more devices were added to the Internet.

In 1981, *The New York Times* began reporting on a new type of crime that had seldom been seen before. It involved stealing top-secret information from computers connected to the Internet. Those behind these early cyberattacks were **rogue** computer experts known as hackers. Just as architects have specialist knowledge in designing buildings, hackers are experts in the **code** used to create computer **software**. To most people, code looks like a random collection of letters and numbers. However, without code, computers would not work. Those letters and numbers are instructions that tell the computer how to perform tasks. Hackers know how to alter code in order to make computers, and the software applications that run on them, behave differently. Some hackers are capable of creating

Al-Qaeda terrorists used the Internet to plan their attack on September 11, 2001, on the Pentagon in Washington, DC.

Hackers often target the Wi-Fi networks in cafés and other public places, in order to spy on the devices of unsuspecting Internet users.

software applications of their own, designed for criminal purposes such as stealing money or spying on other computer users.

In 1988, a new form of criminal software known as a "worm" was used to attack computers in the United States. It was designed to jump from machine to machine over the Internet. Each time it moved to a new device, it altered an important piece of code. Once the worm had infected a computer, that computer became almost unusable. The worm was the work of a hacker named Robert Tappan Morris. Morris said that he created it to try to find out how big the Internet really was. In the years that followed the Morris worm, the number of

cyberattacks by hackers quickly grew. Internet security experts, who try to keep computers safe from hackers, warned that attacks could come from criminal gangs, terrorist groups, political organizations, and even entire countries.

Today, there are more potential targets for cyberattacks than ever before. It is not just home computers, smartphones, and tablets that can be attacked, but anything connected to the Internet. That includes what experts call **critical infrastructure**, such as the network of cables that carries electricity around the country, city traffic lights, and some home appliances, such as smart televisions. In a cyber war, all these things, and more, could come under attack.

In February 1988, three teenagers managed to hack into the computers of a Unites States Air Force base in San Antonio, Texas. The hackers stole passwords and usernames, which allowed them to take a more detailed look at the secret contents of the US military's computer networks. This simple cyberattack scared the US government into action. President Clinton asked the Department of Defense to come up with a cybersecurity plan to protect government and military computers. The US government now takes the threat of cyberattacks very seriously. Since 2003, the Department of Homeland Security has included a Cyber Security Division. It works with the **Federal Bureau of Investigation (FBI)**, **Central Intelligence Agency (CIA)** and **National Security Agency (NSA)** on identifying and combating threats from hackers. In 2006, the Joint Chiefs of Staff released the National Military Strategy for Cyberspace Operations. Three years later, United States Cyber Command (USCYBERCOM) was launched to operate alongside the US Army, Navy, and Air Force.

Many other governments around the world have taken similar measures. They have seen the number of attempted cyberattacks increase every year and have taken action to protect their citizens. Behind closed doors, many governments may also be developing cyberweapons of their own, targeted at other nations. It is because of this that some experts believe that cyber warfare is the biggest threat we face in the twenty-first century.

Bill Clinton was the first US president to acknowledge the threat of cyber war.

I WITNESS WAR

In 2013, James Comey was appointed director of the FBI. Since taking office, he has given evidence to the United States Senate Committee on Homeland Security on a number of occasions. On October 8, 2015, he spoke to the Committee about the threat posed by cyberattacks. He said:

Hackers can activate a virus hidden inside a computer by using a single line of command code.

"An element of virtually every national security threat and crime problem the FBI faces is cyber-based or facilitated. We face sophisticated cyberthreats from state-sponsored hackers, hackers for hire, organized cybersyndicates, and terrorists. On a daily basis, cyber-based actors seek our state secrets, our trade secrets, our technology, and our ideas—things of incredible value to all of us and of great importance to the conduct of our government business and our national security. They seek to strike our critical infrastructure and to harm our economy."

What do you think the "sophisticated cyberthreats" James Comey mentions in this speech are?

What does he mean when he talks about "state-sponsored hackers"?

Read the extract again, and then consider the size of the cyber war threat to the United States.

CHAPTER 2

OPERATION ORCHARD

Around 1 a.m. on September 6, 2007, a bright flash lit up the night sky in the desert outside of Deir el-Zor in Syria. Afterward, a giant column of smoke could be seen stretching up toward the sky. What could have happened in this remote part of the Middle East?

The next afternoon, the Syrian government blamed its neighbor, Israel. It said that Israeli fighter jets had dropped bombs over deserted areas without causing any human or material damage. The government of Israel immediately denied the reports, saying that the incident never occurred. However, something very significant did happen in the desert that night. Over the years that followed, investigative journalists spent countless days, weeks, and months trying to uncover the real story. We now know that those bright flashes were indeed exploding bombs, dropped by Israeli jets. They were targeting what they thought was a top-secret nuclear

Documents stolen by members of the Israeli secret service showed that Syria was planning to develop nuclear missiles like these.

research facility. According to reports, the mission was known as Operation Orchard. It began earlier in the year, when agents from MOSSAD, the Israeli **intelligence** service, broke into the London hotel room of a top Syrian official. They found his laptop, hacked into it, and installed a special piece of software, known as a Trojan horse virus.

A Trojan horse is a software application that is designed to look harmless, but it is, in fact, very dangerous. The computer user will never notice anything different, but secretly, the Trojan horse will be at work. The true purpose of a Trojan is always hidden but usually involves secretly stealing documents or personal information. The Trojan used by MOSSAD spies was designed to steal electronic documents. After studying these documents, the spies found pictures that seemed to prove that Syria was secretly building a **nuclear reactor** deep in the desert. The Israeli government believed that the nuclear reactor was part of a larger Syrian plan to secretly develop **nuclear weapons**. They feared that Syria was trying to build atomic bombs that could destroy Israeli cities such as Jerusalem and Tel Aviv. As a result of this, Israel decided to act.

Israel's Prime Minister, Ehud Olmert, secretly sought approval for the Operation Orchard attack from US President George W. Bush.

On that fateful night in September 2007, Israeli fighter jets dropped around seventeen tons (15.4 metric tons) of explosives on the site near al-Kibar, destroying it completely. The mission was such a success that the Israeli jets were able to fly to Syria and back without being detected. By the time Syrian officials knew what was happening, Israel was already celebrating its success.

The fact that Israel's air attack went undetected is very unusual. Like many countries, Syria uses an electronic early-warning system called **radar** to keep track of what is happening in the skies. Radar systems were first developed in World War II (1939–1945) to alert Britain, the United States, and their **allies** of approaching German aircraft. The system works by sending out radio waves, which bounce off airplanes. By recording how long it takes for these radio waves to return to the radar station, it is possible to calculate the exact position of aircraft in the sky. Radar operators are trained to watch an image on a computer screen and report any unusual, unidentified objects. On September 6, 2007,

Syrian radar operators did not spot anything unusual on their computer screens. Everything appeared calm and normal, with no cause for alarm. As far as they were concerned, the country was safe from attack.

In the months that followed, reports began to appear suggesting that Israel had used a network weapon to trick Syrian radar. According to these reports, Israel was able to take control of the computer software running Syria's early-warning radar system. Once they had done that, they were able to display false pictures, showing no fighter jets flying into Syrian **airspace**. This was a devastating development. Although reports claimed that the US military had been trying

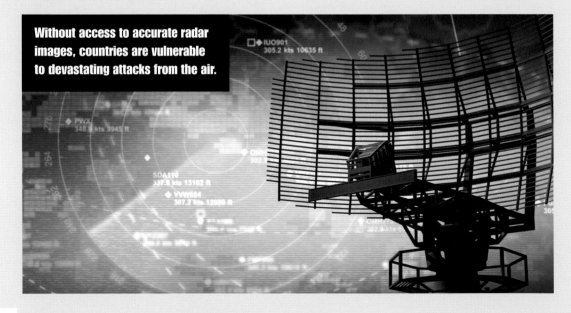

Without access to accurate radar images, countries are vulnerable to devastating attacks from the air.

Hackers are trained to work quickly, striking networks before their targets have a chance to respond.

out similar systems in Iraq and Afghanistan, they had never been used on such a major operation. The era of electronic warfare had arrived.

Operation Orchard had started by a hacking a single Syrian laptop computer and ended with hackers taking control of military radar systems. The bombing that destroyed Syria's nuclear reactor would not have been a success without the use of cutting-edge cyber warfare techniques. To this day, Syria has never confirmed that a nuclear research facility was destroyed in September 2007. Experts say that the Syrian government did not want to admit that it was trying to develop nuclear weapons, possibly with the help of North Korea. Israel, too, has refused to admit its role in the incident, preferring to say that nothing happened.

13

Although what happened in Syria in 2007 has never been confirmed, if news reports are correct, it suggests that national governments may be developing cyberweapons. When journalists have asked government spokespeople if this is the case, they have rarely gotten clear answers. Countries around the world are happy to talk about protecting their citizens against cyberattacks, but they refuse to admit that they carry out cyber war missions of their own.

Any information relating to military action is classified as "top secret," unless governments choose to make it available to the public.

For example, there is much we know about the killing of **Osama bin Laden** on May 2, 2011, because the US government released it. However, only a handful of politicians and military officials know the full story. Similarly, the witnesses most likely to know the full facts of Operation Orchard are those in positions of power within the Israeli and Syrian governments. To date, they have been very careful in what they have said about the mission. However, through studying their words, we may be able to figure out whether Israel was responsible and whether they would use cyberweapons in future.

The NSA's cyberspying teams played a vital role in the hunt for Osama bin Laden, whom US Special Forces killed in May 2011.

I WITNESS WAR

TOP SECRET

Pinhas Buchris is one of Israel's top cybersecurity experts. He spent many years as head of Unit 8200, the cyberdefense arm of the country's military forces. He also worked as commander of a **classified** technology unit. In November 2007, while he was serving as Director General of Israel's Ministry of Defense, he spoke to *Aviation Week & Space Technology* magazine about his country's cyber war strategy:

> "Offensive and defensive network warfare is one of the most interesting new areas. I can only say we're following the [network attack] technology with great care. I doubted this [technology] five years ago. But we did it. Now everything has changed. You need this kind of capability. You're not being responsible if you're not dealing with it. And, if you can build this kind of capability, the sky's the limit."

Details of Operation Orchard may be contained in classified documents prepared by the Israeli and US governments.

What do you think the difference is between "defensive" and "offensive" cyber warfare?

In this context, what do you think "we did it" means? Do you think he is admitting involvement in the Operation Orchard attack or referring to something else?

Based on this extract, do you think Israel is developing cyberweapons capable of targeting countries? Support your answer with a quotation from the extract.

CHAPTER 3

DENIAL OF SERVICE

Since gaining independence from Russian rule in 1991, Estonia has become one of the world's most connected countries. It has pioneered the idea of "e-government," where citizens can access government services, including voting in elections, over the Internet. Over three weeks in May 2007, many of Estonia's most popular websites were temporarily shut down by waves of aggressive cyberattacks.

For a country that had embraced the Internet so enthusiastically, the attacks were very unsettling. The hackers targeted websites belonging to banks, newspapers, Internet companies, the national parliament, and the office of the president. The attacks began a few days after the government moved a statue that was popular with the country's large Russian community. Almost one-quarter of Estonians have some family connection to Russia, and many were not happy that the statue had been moved. They took to the streets of the capital city, Tallinn, to protest. The protests resulted in violent clashes with the police. Almost as soon as the riots died down, the cyberattacks started. The hackers used a technique known as Distributed Denial of Service (DDoS).

Estonians were shocked when hackers attacked the website of the country's parliament in Tallinn, shown here.

The idea behind a DDoS attack is to stop websites from working by flooding them with **connection requests** over a very short period of time. To do this, hackers must first infect a huge number of computers with a Trojan virus. Together, these infected computers are known as a botnet, or zombie army. When the time comes to launch a DDos attack, the hackers send a simple command to all of the infected computers in the botnet. Within seconds, they will overload the targeted website with information requests. Often, DDoS attacks do not cause lasting damage to the websites being targeted, but they do keep members of the public from accessing them.

In the case of Estonia in 2007, the attacks meant that hundreds of thousands of Estonians could not access their Internet banking, find out the latest news, or use important government websites. When the Estonian government began to investigate the source of the DDoS attacks, they soon discovered that they came from Russia. They also found instructions on how to conduct attacks on a number of Russian websites. The Russian government strenuously denied all involvement.

In a DDoS attack, a single website server is targeted by many different computers at the same time.

The cybersecurity experts who investigated the DDoS attacks in Estonia were in no doubt that Russia was behind them. Other countries, though, were careful not to lay the blame at President Putin's door for fear of retaliation by Russia. The three-week incident has since been described as the first-known case of a nation-state targeting another by cyber warfare. Over the years that followed, a number of similar incidents have occurred, but these happened just before fighting broke out on the ground.

In the summer of 2008, the relationship between Georgia and neighbor Russia was at an all-time low. Since becoming an independent nation following the fall of the Russia-dominated Soviet Union in the early 1990s, Georgia had gone through several periods of **civil war**. In 2008, those troubles resurfaced, with Russian-speaking Georgians in the Abkhazia and South Ossettia regions demanding closer links with Russia. As Russia and Georgia edged closer to war, the cyberattacks started.

Following the cyberattacks and Russian invasion, thousands of Georgians took to the streets in support of their government.

The Russian invasion, which featured fleets of military trucks, was a show of strength by President Putin.

In late July, cybersecurity experts started noticing a wave of distributed DDoS attacks aimed at Georgian government websites. A botnet was again responsible, firing out hundreds of thousands of website connection requests a second. Each request was accompanied by a message written into the code: "win+love+in+Russia." The website of the Georgian president could not handle the attack and was taken off-line for more than twenty-four hours. As a war between Georgia and its powerful neighbor drew ever closer, the attacks continued. On August 8, 2008, intense fighting between Russian and Georgian forces in the South Ossettia province broke out. Governments worldwide called for calm, fearing that Russia would not stop until Georgia surrendered. By August 13, a **ceasefire** had been agreed upon.

What happened in Georgia in 2008 is now thought to be significant. Experts say that it marked the first time that cyber warfare attacks had coincided with a traditional war. Georgia accused Russia of being behind the cyberattacks, and as to be expected, Russia said it was not to blame. Whether Russia was responsible or not, it would not be the last time that cyberattacks had coincided with Russian military action.

Since November 2013, Ukraine has been involved in a bloody civil war. The country's president was forced out of office following months of protest, before Russian-speaking Ukrainians in the east of the country decided to push for independence. Many experts believe that Russia is backing these eastern **rebels**. In the middle of it all, Russia invaded Crimea, an area of Ukraine that includes an important military port. Many years ago, Crimea was part of the Soviet Union, and President Putin vowed to return it to Russia.

The Ukraine Crisis, as it has become known, is a very modern war. From the start, there has been evidence of cyber warfare. According to one report, cyberattacks have been targeted at government websites and Internet servers, as well as the smartphones, tablets, and computers of leading protesters. Hackers have also used the Internet to spread false information and to spy on the Ukrainian Army. Some of the most serious incidents were timed to coincide with the shooting of anti-Russian protesters.

After capturing Sevastopol harbor on the Crimean coast, Russian forces could surround Ukraine in the event of a war between the two nations.

In the future, cyberattacks will be as common a feature of warfare as tanks, fighter planes, and missiles.

I WITNESS WAR

Glib Pakharenko is a cybersecurity expert living in Kiev, the capital city of Ukraine. He has seen the crisis in the country unfold close at hand. In 2015, he wrote an article on cyber warfare during the ongoing crisis. In it, Pakharenko laid out the evidence he has gathered, which points to Russian state involvement in hacking and cyberattacks. He wrote:

"The world should not underestimate Russia, which is seeking to re-establish its former empire, to include Ukraine and other parts of the defunct Soviet Union and Warsaw Pact. In the context of its wide-ranging political and military campaigns, Russia has developed a cyberattack capability that can target national critical infrastructures, via the Internet, anywhere in the world."

Use a dictionary to find out what an empire is. Do you think there is evidence that Russia is trying to create one in the twenty-first century?

What was the Warsaw Pact? Do some research to find out more, and then consider whether Russia would like to return to this state of affairs.

Based on this extract, how dangerous do you think Russia's cyberattack capability is to world peace?

CHAPTER 4

STEALING SECRETS

Most incidents of computer hacking are not acts of cyber war. Instead, many hackers are criminals who create dangerous software applications, such as Trojan viruses and worms, in order to steal information from computer users.

The sort of information these criminal hackers are looking for varies, but it often includes bank account numbers, credit card data, and Internet passwords. Criminals can then use these to try to steal money or to sell the information on to larger criminal gangs. The kind of cyberweapons used by criminal hackers are designed for spying on unsuspecting computer users. They can use viruses to create keyloggers, which keep a record of everything a person types, or to switch on webcams to listen in on video calls.

Chinese hackers are thought to be behind hundreds of cyberattacks on US businesses every year.

As the world's largest Internet company, Google is often a target of cyberattacks.

Experts say that these kinds of online spying techniques are also used by agencies such as the NSA, Britain's Government Communication Headquarters (GCHQ), Israel's Unit 8200, and Russia's Federal Security Sevices (FSB). Spying like this is known as cyberespionage, and it forms an important part of the intelligence gathering process. Spy agencies are incredibly secretive about their activities. Although we do not know what they do, former spies claim that these agencies often employ expert hackers. On rare occasions, research by cybersecurity experts also uncovers evidence of spying by groups of hackers with links to spy agencies.

In January 2010, Google, one of the world's biggest Internet companies, announced that it had been targeted by a "highly sophisticated and targeted" cyberattack. The hackers managed to steal **intellectual property** from the company. They also tried to access the e-mail accounts of a number of people known for protesting against the Chinese government. Google went on to state that these hackers had targeted at least twenty other large US corporations. Three years later, former US government officials spoke to journalists about the incident. They said that a group of hackers linked to the Chinese army carried out the attacks. The hackers were trying to access Gmail accounts that were being monitored by the FBI. If they could access this information, then they could find out if any of their undercover spies were being investigated. This major cyberespionage attack was known as Operation Aurora. It was named for the Aurora Trojan virus the hackers used. China has denied any involvement in the attacks.

In May 2013, twenty-nine-year-old NSA employee, Edward Snowden, boarded a flight from Hawaii to Hong Kong. When he arrived in Hong Kong, Snowden contacted an investigative journalist and invited him to a secret meeting. He had important information he wanted to share. Snowden told the reporter that he had hard drives full of classified documents that proved that the US government and its allies had been using the Internet to spy, not only on suspected criminals, but also on innocent members of the public. Snowden wanted to share this information, becoming one of the most famous **whistle-blowers** in history. The US government called Snowden a traitor.

To this day, Edward Snowden remains in hiding, afraid for his safety. The documents he gave to reporters proved that the United States had spied on the leaders of the Brazilian and German governments, and collected telephone-call records for millions of Americans, as well as the Internet histories of many people around the world. Since Edward Snowden's revelations, cybersecurity experts and journalists have found links between dangerous computer viruses, known as malware, and the NSA.

Five years after revealing the extent of cyberespionage by the US government, Edward Snowden was still in hiding.

In 2015, German newspaper *Der Spiegel* ran a story about a famous piece of malware known as Regin. Regin had been discovered some years earlier and was described by Internet security company Symantec as a "complex intelligence gathering and surveillance tool." Infections of the Regin malware were found in computers across the world. Regin was used to spy on governments,

Following Snowden's revelations, protestors took to the streets of Washington, DC, to demand an end to cybersurveillance.

WE CAN STOP MASS SPYING
DEFEND CONSTITUTIONAL RIGHTS!

businesses, university researchers, and individuals. *Der Spiegel* analyzed the computer code used by Regin and found that it was very similar to other malware viruses allegedly developed by the NSA and GCHQ. They said that Regin was so complicated and advanced that it would have taken years to develop. It was designed to hide inside infected computers for years on end.

This was not the first time that the US government had been linked to sophisticated malware. In 2012, *The Washington Post* reported that the NSA, CIA, and Israel's military had used another dangerous software virus known as Flame to spy on Iran. It is now thought that Regin and Flame were part of a larger campaign code-named "Operation Olympic Games."

The newspaper revelations about who was behind the dangerous Regin and Flame malware viruses made many people around the world really think about cyber war for the first time. Their discovery followed on from high-profile cyberattacks on US companies by Chinese hackers and the possible Russian use of malware. Together, these incidents suggested that cyber warfare was much more widespread than anyone had previously thought. The revelations also showed that countries across the globe were investing time and money in hacking, either to spy on people or to weaken other nations. Some experts began calling for an international **peace treaty** to try to stop the use of cyberweapons. In the past, peace treaties have been used to control the use of dangerous weapons, such as nuclear missiles. Could a cyber war peace treaty be the answer?

The United Nations (UN) headquarters is based in New York City. The UN believes that countries must work together to prevent cyber war.

I WITNESS WAR

From 2007 to 2014, Dr. Hamadoun Toure was the Secretary General of the International Telecommunications Union (ITU). The ITU is an organization set up by the UN to promote peaceful cooperation between countries around communication technology. This includes telephone networks and the Internet. In August 2012, Dr. Toure gave a speech where he discussed the growing threat of cyber war:

"With malware and cyberweapons, we have seen how the power of Information Communication Technology (ICT) networks acts as a lure to terrorism and espionage, shaping a new concept of war – cyber war. Cyber war is launched in cyberspace, but it can quickly spread beyond the virtual world, affecting governments, businesses, and individuals. We need to start thinking seriously about the potential global negative impact that this may have on international security, and to put aside any political or other differences. Malicious cyberactivities pose high-level threats to national security. Without secure individuals and secure countries, we cannot hope to achieve international security."

What is cyberspace? Do some research, and then write your own explanation as to what Dr. Toure means.

What does "malicious" mean? Do you think software viruses such as Flame and Regin are malicious?

After reading this extract, do you think it will be possible for countries to agree not to use cyberweapons in the future?

27

CHAPTER 5

OPERATION OLYMPIC GAMES

In June 2010, a cybersecurity expert named Sergey Ulasen was asked by his boss to look at a customer's computer. The computer had started behaving very strangely. Little did Sergey Ulasen know this was the beginning of one of the most explosive cyber warfare stories of all time.

When Ulasen began investigating, he was shocked by what he found. A previously undiscovered computer worm had worked its way into the computer. Ulasen studied it further. Over the hours that followed, he realized that it was one of the most dangerous pieces of malware he had ever seen. He had to warn other cybersecurity experts about what he had found. Soon, the aggressive worm was found on computers all over the world. Little over a month after Ulasen stumbled across it, the malware had made its way into fifty thousand computers. Large Internet-security companies Kaspersky Lab and Symantec worked around the clock to try to find a way to stop this worm. They also gave the worm a name: Stuxnet.

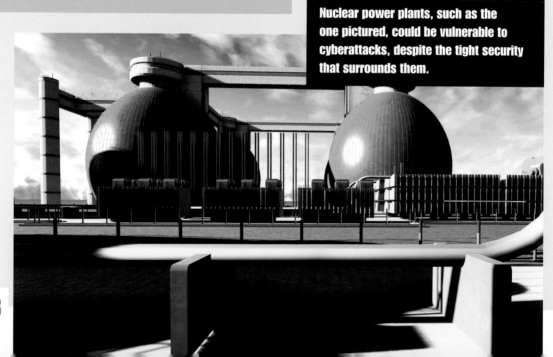

Nuclear power plants, such as the one pictured, could be vulnerable to cyberattacks, despite the tight security that surrounds them.

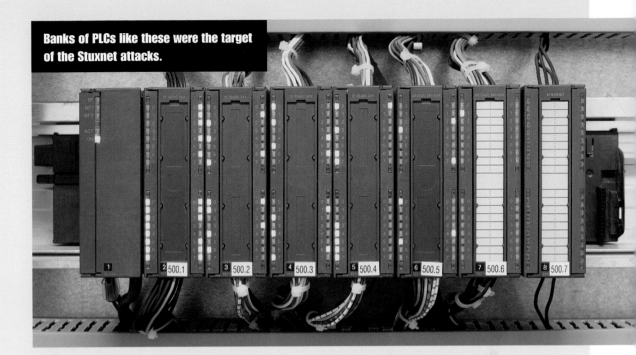

Banks of PLCs like these were the target of the Stuxnet attacks.

While studying the Stuxnet worm, they found out that it could copy itself onto any device connected to an infected computer. That means that it could infect portable hard drives, such as USB sticks, as well as computers connected to a network such as the Internet. Although Stuxnet infected huge numbers of computers, it appeared not to damage them. Eventually, researchers figured out that the malware had been designed to damage a very specific type of computer known as a Programmable Logic Controller (PLC). These are specialist devices often found in factories and power plants, usually connected to a control computer running Microsoft Windows.

Even more interestingly, Stuxnet was supposed to harm only a certain type of PLC made by a company called Siemens. The worm's code told it to seek out the software used to run these particular PLCs and told it to behave differently. The researchers were confused: Who would want to target this type of PLC, and why? Something else was troubling the experts, too. The Stuxnet worm was incredibly complicated, suggesting that a single hacker could not have created it. This led experts to conclude that it must have been the work of a government or states working together. They had discovered one of the most devastating cyberweapon the world had ever seen.

Stuxnet had first been discovered on a computer in Iran and had infected computers in companies with links to the country's top-secret nuclear program. As a result of this, experts concluded that it could only have been the work of a group of countries that wanted to stop or slow down Iran's nuclear ambitions. The United States, Israel, and the United Kingdom were the main suspects. As you would expect, none of these countries has ever admitted responsibility for creating the Stuxnet worm. However, thanks to years of research from investigative journalists such as *Wired* magazine's Kim Zetter and documentary filmmaker Alex Gibney, there is enough evidence to suggest that

Stuxnet was developed as part of a secret campaign to damage Iran's nuclear program. The campaign was codenamed Operation Olympic Games. The Stuxnet worm was able to infect Windows computers because those behind it, thought to be the NSA and Unit 8200, had used weaknesses they had discovered in popular software applications. These weaknesses, or holes, are known as zero-day vulnerabilities. They are so rare that even the companies that wrote the software usually do not know about them. Stuxnet reportedly targeted more than one zero-day vulnerability. Experts now believe that Stuxnet was designed to find and infect PLCs inside the Netanz nuclear facility in Iran.

Qatari energy firm RasGas had to shut down its computer systems following a massive cyberattack in August 2012.

Iranian computer engineers took several months to figure out the source of the problems at the Netanz nuclear facility.

The virus probably got into the control computers through an infected USB stick brought into the facility by a worker. Once there, it could finally begin to perform the task it was designed for.

Iran was using PLCs to control the spinning **centrifuges** that turn uranium into usable nuclear fuel. The Stuxnet worm made the centrifuges spin so fast that they broke. At the same time, it fed false information to the control computers. This information said that everything was running smoothly. In truth, the cyberattack had severely damaged Iran's nuclear program. It would take years to repair the damage.

Today, many people believe that both the Stuxnet worm and the attack on Netanz were part of Operation Olympic Games. By studying documents revealed by Edward Snowden (see page 24), cybersecurity experts have shown links between the Regin and Flame malware, which were used for spying, and the Stuxnet cyberweapon. Iran clearly thought that the United States and Israel were to blame for the attack. In the following years, the Iranian Cyber Army was created. Some believe the Iranian Cyber Army is linked to the Iranian government. This hacking group has claimed responsibility for attacks on US banks, a Las Vegas casino, and a gas company in Qatar.

On August 15, 2012, one of the world's leading oil companies, Saudi Aramco, was hit by a massive cyberattack. A dangerous piece of malware known as Shamoon quickly spread throughout the company's network of computers. Like Stuxnet, the Shamoon worm was able to make copies of itself in order to infect a huge number of machines. Shamoon was designed to destroy computers from the inside. In total, more than thirty thousand computers belonging to Saudi Aramco were damaged, most beyond repair.

The attack on Saudi Aramco has been called the single biggest hack in history. The size of the cyberattack suggests that a country's government, rather than a small group of independent hackers, was responsible. But which country would do this? Saudi Aramco is owned by the Saudi Arabian government, and Saudi Arabia and the United States are known allies. As a result of this, most experts concluded that the attack could have been a revenge attack by the Iranian Cyber Army.

Following the attack on its computer systems, Saudi Aramco had to scrap thousands of computers.

I WITNESS WAR

Before e-mail became popular, businesses would send and receive important documents using fax machines.

Chris Kubecka is an Internet security expert and researcher who lives in the Netherlands. She owns and runs a company called Hypasec, which specialises in responding to cyberattacks and investigating digital crimes, such as hacking. Following the attacks on Saudi Aramco, the company hired her to help rebuild their network and create security teams. She told us:

"The attack was horrible. Saudi Aramco told me to hire the best people I could, because they needed to fix the problems quickly. When I started, it was still extremely chaotic. They had to take tens of thousands of computers off-line and do business the old way, with typewriters and fax machines. On the day of the attack, they had Internet, phone, and e-mail access. By the afternoon, they had no modern technology. To make matters worse, the attacks kept going for months afterward. The attackers were taunting us. The easy conclusion to come to was that Iran was behind it, but the evidence is circumstantial."

What are typewriters and fax machines? How would using this kind of technology compare to using modern computers?

Chris says that the attackers were "taunting" Saudi Aramco. Why would the hackers do this?

What is circumstantial evidence? Look up the meaning of the term, and then think about whether we should believe reports that Iran was responsible for the attacks.

CHAPTER 6

CHANGING THE WORLD

North Korea regularly threatens to attack neighboring countries, both with traditional military methods and cyber warfare techniques.

There are many different reasons why hackers undertake cyberattacks. Some are motivated by money and will work for whoever offers to pay them the most. Others are employed by governments to help them spy on other countries. Some may just want to show off their code-breaking skills or are simply interested in reading classified documents.

A hacker named Gary McKinnon, who managed to access top-secret US military computer systems, claimed that he was trying to find evidence of unidentified flying objects (UFOs). McKinnon's attacks were so successful that the US government had to shut down more than two thousand computers for twenty-four hours. Due to illness, McKinnon has never stood trial for his crimes. If he was ever convicted, he could spend up to sixty years in jail. Another famous cyberattack apparently came about because one man really did not like people making fun of him. The man in question was Kim Jong-un,

the president of North Korea. Kim Jong-un did not want people to see a movie called *The Interview*, which is a comedy about two CIA agents trying to kill the North Korean president. In an attempt to stop the movie from being released, he ordered a group of North Korean hackers to attack the computer systems of Sony Pictures, the company making the movie. The hackers called themselves Guardians of Peace. Using malware, they managed to steal a large number of top-secret documents, as well as digital copies of a number of Sony-made movies that had yet to be released. They leaked all of this online and then threatened to attack screenings of *The Interview*. Sony canceled plans to release the movie.

Changing the way people think about a particular issue can also motivate hackers. In 2016, a group of Russian hackers known as Fancy Bears carried out a successful attack on the world Anti-Doping Agency (WADA). This is the organization that oversees drug testing of professional athletes. Months before the attack, many Russian athletes had been banned from competing in the 2016 Olympic Games in Rio for taking performance-enhancing drugs. In the cyberattack on WADA, the Fancy Bears stole drug testing and medical records for a number of high-profile UK and US athletes. The hackers then posted these records online for everyone to see. The documents showed that some athletes had obtained permission to take certain banned substances to treat medical conditions. The hackers wanted to harm the athletes' careers and suggested that it was not just the Russians who tried to bend the rules.

The process of stealing information and then making it available to the public, often by giving it to newspapers or television stations, is known as leaking. The documents leaked are usually top secret and contain information that powerful politicians, governments, companies, and celebrities do not want other people to know about. Hackers who use cyberattacks to steal and leak sensitive documents often say that they do it to change the way people think. If you can change the way people think about a subject, then they may change the way they behave. Having read these top-secret documents, people might vote for a different candidate in an election, organize protests against the government, or stop buying products made by a particular company. Hackers who use cyberattacks for these reasons call themselves "hacktivists." They see themselves as protesters. Instead of organizing demonstrations or writing to their senator, they use illegal cyber warfare techniques to raise awareness of issues that concern them.

The world's largest and most famous group of hacktivists calls itself Anonymous. Anonymous was formed in 2003 and has been responsible for many cyberattacks.

To hide their identities, hackers from Anonymous wear these distinctive masks when they appear in public.

In 2011, billboards supporting the controversial website, Wikileaks, began appearing in Los Angeles, California.

Anonymous is famous for shutting down websites and releasing YouTube videos explaining why they have done so. Their members are known for wearing distinctive Guy Fawkes masks. Over the years, Anonymous has claimed responsibility for cyberattacks on the Church of Scientology, music and movie industry organizations, the World Trade Organization, and some of President Trump's businesses. They say they have also released information on criminals who target children and the terrorist group ISIS. After ISIS terrorists carried out an attack in Paris in 2015, Anonymous declared cyber war on the group.

When Anonymous and other hacktivist groups manage to steal top-secret information, they often pass it on to a website called Wikileaks. Since it was set up in 2006, Wikileaks has shared millions of top-secret documents. The website features many of the documents stolen by whistle-blower Edward Snowden and Guardians of the Peace. Wikileaks founder, Julian Assange, says that he is promoting freedom of speech, a right protected by the US constitution. His supporters say that the website shows how politicians and government officials act behind closed doors. Opponents dispute this. They say that by releasing secret information, such as intelligence reports by spies, Wikileaks is making the world a much more dangerous place.

When the 2016 United States presidential election campaign began, most experts thought that Democratic Party candidate Hillary Clinton would easily beat her opponent, now President, Republican Donald Trump. Things started to change in June 2016, when *The Washington Post* reported a cyberattack on the Internet servers of the Democratic Party. The newspaper said the hack was the work of two groups with links to the Russian government, Cozy Bear and Fancy Bears. Less than a day later, a hacker calling himself Guccifer 2.0 took to social media to claim that he was behind the attack. To try to prove his version of events, the hacker released a number of private e-mail messages sent by members of Hillary Clinton's campaign team. A month later, twenty thousand e-mails stolen from Democratic Party computers appeared on the Wikileaks website. As the November election date approached, more stolen documents appeared on the Internet. Just eleven days before the polling booths opened, FBI Director James Comey said that he was opening a new investigation into Hillary Clinton. He wanted to see if she had broken the law by using a private e-mail address to send, receive, and store top-secret government documents during her time as President Obama's Secretary

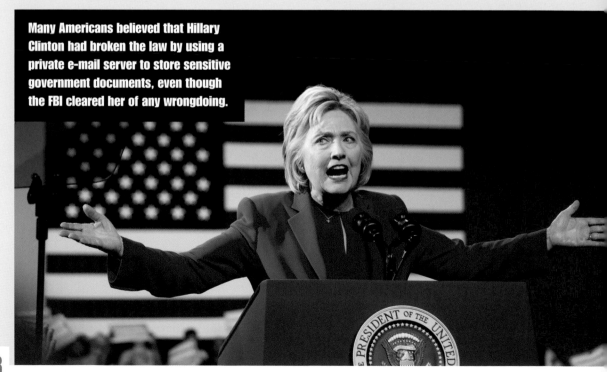

Many Americans believed that Hillary Clinton had broken the law by using a private e-mail server to store sensitive government documents, even though the FBI cleared her of any wrongdoing.

Since taking office, President Trump has repeatedly denied claims of secret links to the Russian government.

of State. It was one of the biggest news stories in the history of US politics. During his candidacy, President Trump accused Hillary Clinton of breaking the law. He said that she was untrustworthy and not fit to be president. Two days before the election, James Comey announced that Clinton had not broken the law. By then, the damage had been done. On November 9, 2016, it was announced that Donald Trump had won the election and would become the next president of the United States.

Many experts believed that the hacked e-mails shared by Wikileaks damaged Hillary Clinton's election campaign. They said that whoever was behind the attack wanted Trump to become president. They thought that without these leaks, Trump would have lost. So who was really behind the cyberattack? Julian Assange, the founder of Wikileaks, said he did not know who had given his website the hacked e-mails. He pointed out that most of the hackers who pass Wikileaks information do it **anonymously**. They think that if they reveal their identities, their lives may be in danger.

In January 2017, the US government said that it had proof that Russia was behind the Democratic Party cyberattacks. They said this top-secret information showed that President Putin ordered a campaign of attacks against the Democratic Party and Hillary Clinton's presidential campaign. In its opinion, Russian hackers had done this to give Donald Trump a better chance of being elected president. Not everyone agreed with these findings. Critics said that the report was missing the kind of technical evidence needed to prove that Russia was to blame. The US government responded by saying that evidence did exist, but that it was classified to ensure national security. Some cybersecurity experts still question the government's findings. They say that the cyber warfare techniques used in the attack are popular with a wide range of hackers, not just those with links to Russia's spy service. Critics point out that the Democratic Party did not use cybersecurity to protect its e-mails. That means that almost any hacker in the world could have stolen them. Unless the US government releases all of the evidence it has, we may never know for sure whether Russia was really behind the attacks.

This building is the home of Russian intelligence service, the FSB, which the US government says has carried out many cyberattacks against US targets.

I WITNESS WAR

Robert Graham is the Chief Executive Officer of Internet-security firm Errata Security. Following the 2016 presidential election, he wrote a number of blog posts analyzing the government's response to the cyberattacks on the Democratic Party. In them, he looked at the evidence and drew his own conclusions. In posts from December 2016, he wrote:

Coding experts use their skills to help companies protect their computer systems are known as "white hat hackers."

"It's not that Russia isn't involved, it's that the exact nature of their involvement is complicated. Just because the hackers live in Russia doesn't automatically mean that their attacks are directed by the government. The facts we actually see is an attack no more sophisticated than those conducted by Anonymous. We see an attack that is disorganized and opportunistic. Putin's regime may be involved, and they may have a plan, but the current evidence looks like casual hackers, not professional hackers working for an intelligence service."

Graham says that the story is "complicated." What do you think he means?

What makes the attack opportunistic? Who would have the opportunity to carry out such an attack, and why?

Based on this quote, do you think that there is enough evidence to prove that the Russian government ordered the attacks?

If you are waging a war against a much more powerful enemy, it is unlikely that you will have enough soldiers, guns, or bombs to win a traditional war. However, you may be able to win a cyber war. Attacking computers costs very little compared to how much it costs to buy weapons. For this reason, terrorist groups have begun to use cyberattacks against their enemies. Terrorist groups are very dangerous. They believe in a cause so strongly that they are willing to do almost anything, including killing innocent people, to achieve their aims.

Cyberterrorism is thought to be a growing threat. Since 2014, hackers who support the Islamic terrorist group ISIS have claimed responsibility for a number of cyberattacks. In January 2015, the group hacked into the social media accounts of US Central Command, which is responsible for US military activities in the Middle East. The hackers changed pictures and posted tweets that appeared to include classified information. It was not the first time that major cyberattacks had been linked to Islamic terrorist groups.

Although Israel and Hamas agreed to stop fighting in late January 2009, the two sides are still at war online.

ISIS, the Islamic terror organization behind the 2015 attacks in Paris, France, now has a cyber war division.

In January 2009, Israel launched a major bombing offensive in the Gaza Strip, a tightly controlled area in the Palestinian Territory. Israel said that the Palestinians had been attacking Israel with rocket-fire, and it wanted to stop it. Soon after the bombing began, a number of Israeli government websites were hit by a wave of DDoS attacks. Reports say that the hackers used a botnet made up of millions of infected computers to launch the attack. Israeli government officials believed that Islamic groups Hezbollah and Hamas paid Russian hackers to attack Israel. They also said that it was not the first time that hackers linked to Islamic terror groups had attempted to attack Israeli websites.

Many people think that cyberterrorism will be a growing threat to our security in the future. They point out that terrorist groups can seek out experienced criminal hackers and pay them to carry out attacks on their behalf. The FBI thinks that the groups such as ISIS and Hezbollah may try to use the same criminal hacking groups with links to the Russian and Iranian governments. After the 2015 ISIS terror attacks in Paris, hacking group Anonymous said that it would target hackers connected with the terrorist organization, including the so-called "cybercaliphate" that attacked US Central Command.

It is difficult to assess the extent of cyber war and how much of a threat it is to our security. It is a new theater of conflict that features "soldiers" with many different aims. Hackers know how to cover their tracks, making it increasingly difficult to find out who is really behind an attack or cyber war campaign. In the last twenty years, the number and frequency of cyberattacks has grown rapidly.

Internet security experts have discovered all manner of dangerous software applications, designed either to allow hackers to spy on us or to damage our computers.

We rely on the Internet and connected computer technology more than we have ever done before. As the world becomes even more connected, the number of potential cyber war targets increases.

Hackers often try to attack data centers, which are buildings that host large numbers of storage computers.

Internet security companies will have to work hard to protect our computers, tablets, smartphones, and other connected devices from attack.

Before he left office, President Obama asked the CIA to prepare for cyber war with Russia. While US government plans may change, it is clear that cyber warfare is a continuing threat to the security of the United States.

e Internet continues to play ater role in our day-to-day the number of attempted attacks will increase.

WAR STORY

To find out more information about cyber warfare and to consider some of the issues raised by the conflict, write your own eye-witness account of an event mentioned in this book.

1. Which event will you choose? You could perhaps focus on the Stuxnet attacks, the 2012 attack on Saudi Aramco, or the hacking of the Democratic Party e-mail servers.

2. Research your chosen event. Since many of the events are recent, you should find up-to-date information on the Internet. If you are going to search the Internet, make sure you get an adult to help.

3. From what point of view will you write your account? You could chose to be a hacker, a government spy, a cybersecurity expert, a hackitivist, or a whistle-blower like Edward Snowden.

4. Finally, what format will you use? Your account could be a speech like those by James Comey and Dr. Hamadoun Toure featured earlier in this book. Or it could be an account given to a journalist. It could also be a blog post, such as the one Robert Graham used on page 41.

GLOSSARY

airspace The area of sky above a country that is under the control of that nation.

allies Countries that help one another.

anonymously To do something without taking credit for it or allowing others to know you were responsible.

ceasefire An agreement to stop fighting.

Central Intelligence Agency (CIA) The branch of the US intelligence services tasked with gathering information to protect the security of US citizens.

centrifuges Machines found in nuclear power plants that separate substances.

civil war A conflict between different groups in the same country, usually for control of the government.

classified Available only to authorized people.

code Instructions in the form of letters and numbers given to a computer, so that it can perform tasks.

connection requests The processes a computer goes through every time it accesses a website or web page.

critical infrastructure Services that are essential to the smooth running of a country, such as water and gas pipes, power lines, and telephone lines.

Federal Bureau of Investigation (FBI) The branch of the US intelligence services than investigates crimes within the United States.

intellectual property Ideas, plans, or creative works protected by law.

intelligence Information gathered on people and events around the world.

National Security Agency (NSA) The branch of the US intelligence services tasked with collecting electronic information and telephone communications.

network A collection of connected electronic devices.

nuclear reactor A machine used to create and control nuclear energy.

nuclear weapons Explosive devices that get their force from nuclear reactions.

Osama bin Laden The former leader of the terrorist group al-Qaeda.

peace treaty A formal agreement between nations that officially ends a war.

radar A way of finding the position of an object by bouncing a radio wave off it and analyzing the reflected wave.

rebels Groups of people who refuse to abide by the laws set out by the government of a nation.

rogue Any person or organization that no longer abides by the rules.

software An application, or program, used to perform tasks on a computer.

United Nations (UN) An international organization with 193 independent states as members.

virus Piece of computer code or software application that is loaded onto a computer without consent.

whistle-blowers People who reveal corruption or wrongdoing.

FURTHER READING

BOOKS

Anniss, Matt. *Espionage* (Crime Science). New York, NY: Gareth Stevens Publishing, 2013.

Lassieur, Allison. *Cyber Spies & Secret Agents of Modern Times*. North Mankota, MN: Compass Point Books, 2017.

Loh-Hagan, Virginia. *Ethical Hacker* (Odd Jobs). Ann Arbor, MI: 45th Parallel Press, 2015.

Mitra, Amanda. *Digital Security: Cyber Terror and Cyber Security*. New York, NY: Chelsea House Publishers, 2010.

Parks, Peggy J. *Computer Hacking* (Crime Scene Investigations). San Diego, CA: Lucent Books, 2008.

WEBSITES

ABC Splash
http://www.splash.abc.net.au/home#!/media/2210884/how-do-computers-get-hacked
Watch this video to find out more about how computers get hacked.

Carnegie Cyber Academy
http://www.carnegiecyberacademy.com/facultyPages/cyberCriminals/operate.html
Find out how cybercriminals operate, how they are caught, and the identities of those on cybercrime's most wanted list.

Khan Academy
http://www.khanacademy.org/partner-content/nova/cybersecurity
Read information on cybersecurity, including steps you can take to protect your computer from viruses.

INDEX

Acknowledgments:
The publisher would like to thank the following people for permission to use their material:
p. 9 Excerpt from testimony given by FBI Director James Comey to the US Senate Committee for Homeland Security
& Governmental Affairs, October 8, 2015, p. 15 Pinchas Buchris quoted by David A Fulghum and Robert Wall, "Israel
Shows Electronic Prowess," November 26, 2007, Aviation Week, www.aviationweek.com, p. 21 Glib Pakharenko, "Cyber
Operations at Maidan: A First Hand Account," from the NATO CCD COE publication "Cyber War in Perspective: Russian
Aggression Against Ukraine," edited by Kenneth Greers, www.ccdcoe.org, p. 29 Dr. Hamadoun Toure, ITU Secretary-
General, "Cyber-Resiliance: The Essence of Cyber-Peace," speech to the Erice International Seminars on Planetary
Emergencies, August, 20 2012, Erice, Sicily, Italy, www.itu.int, p. 35 Chris Kubecka, in conversation with the author,
February 1, 2017, p. 43 Robert Graham, "From Putin With Love—A Novel by the New York Times," December 21, 2016,
posted on http://blog.erratsec.com.